Rule
of
Thumb

**A Small Business Guide to
Sustainability**

Rule of Thumb

A Small Business Guide to Sustainability

Dr. Beverly Ann Browning

Text Copyright © 2013 Dr. Beverly Ann Browning

Published by

WriteLife, LLC
2323 S. 171 St.
Suite 202
Omaha, NE 68130

Rule of Thumb
3838 Davenport St
Lower Level
Omaha, NE 68131

www.writelife.com

http://ruleofthumbbiz.com

Printed in the United States of America

ISBN 978 1 60808 053 3

First Edition

Contents

Why Rule of Thumb?

This book is part of the Rule of Thumb series produced in affiliation with the Rule of Thumb for Business whose mission is to "enrich business growth and development." The Rule of Thumb series offers basic information in plain language that will help you start, grow and sustain your business. The explanation for using the *"rule of thumb"* concept was introduced in the first book and is included again here.

Throughout history, a *"rule of thumb"* was used in measurements in a wide variety of businesses and vocations. The following list gives a few examples of how the thumb was used for measuring:

- In agriculture, the thumb was used to measure the depth at which to plant a seed.
- In restaurants and pubs, the thumb was used to measure the temperature of beer and ale.
- Tailors used the thumb to make sure enough space was allowed between the person's skin and his/her clothing. For example, the space between the cuff of the sleeve and the wrist had to be at least the width of the thumb.

- Carpenters used the width of the thumb rather than a ruler for measuring. For example, a notch in a board may need to be cut two thumb widths from the edge.

A *"rule of thumb"* is an idea or rule that may be applied in most situations, but not all. The *"rules of thumb"* in this book give you many reliable, convenient and simple rules that will help you remember many "dos" and "don'ts" that go with owning and running a business. Many of these concepts can also be used in a variety of business situations ranging from management, sales, customer service, human resources and leadership. The information is designed to be easy, simple and action-oriented. To learn more about the Rule of Thumb for Business organization visit our website at www.ruleofthumbbiz.com. – *Rule of Thumb for Business.*

Chapter 1
Sustaining a Small Business:
Getting Started What is Business Sustainability?

Sustainability is a strategy that <u>drives long-term business growth and profitability</u>. Keeping a small business operating after the start-up phase is a major challenge for small businesses across the country. According to CNN (May 20, 2011), across the United States, small business failure rates rose by 40% between 2007 and 2010, according to the report. Only two-thirds of new small businesses survive at least two years, and just 44 percent survive at least four years, according to a study by the U.S. Small Business Association. Even businesses with substantial start-up funds flail around in a brutal economic climate. Those that survived either cut back severely on expenditures or filed for bankruptcy court protection allowing them to pay off creditors over a longer period of time. Staying solvent means enduring or weathering bad times. Surviving all closure odds and trends means that the survivors had a sustainability plan.

How can I adopt a sustainability mind-set?

Strategizing for sustainability involves understanding and adopting the following *stay in business* mind-set:

1. **Eliminating Visioning Barriers.** Focus on being mentally prepared for staying in business beyond the finish line. This means closing your ears to all naysayers who didn't believe that you could start a business early on and now are waiting to give you bad advice about how to run your business and stay in business.

2. **Sharpening Your Vision.** Hone your ability to visualize business success in order to produce more confident actions. Increased confidence about business sustainability breeds success. This means letting go of everyone in your circle of colleagues and friends that don't share your vision. Controlling the environment that you manage and growing your business is critical to sustainability.

3. **Welcoming Sacrifice.** Accept the fact that business success does not come without sacrifice of self, other human sources, and personal/business finances. This means adopting the "failure is not an option" mind-set to achieve and sustain your dream of a successful business venture.

4. **Learning to Take Risks.** Draw from the actions of earlier successful entrepreneurs who dynamited their way to the top of the Fortune 500 corporations list. Corporate visionaries such as Bill Gates, Warren Buffet, and others realized early on that success comes to those who recognize and take risks, are unafraid of risk, and are willing to execute based on their own ideas (driving visions). This means that if you are a risk avoider, your chances of business survival (aka sustainability) will probably be slim.

5. **Creating Something Out of Nothing.** When clients and customers are few and far between, revenues are less or nonexistent. This means that you must be able to pattern your actions like the actions of the business owners that have already achieved long-term business sustainability. Think outside of the usual box for operating your business and create a plan for drumming up new revenues.

6. **Drawing Up a Sustainability Roadmap.** Remember the questions that I asked you under *How Can This Book Help Me?* Carefully thinking about your responses and writing them down constitutes your own customized sustainability plan. This means you must read the rest of this book so you have a working desktop guide on how to achieve

business sustainability, also known as how to beat the odds!

Rule of Thumb:
Look for like-minded entrepreneurs and owners of businesses that have lasted 10 years or more and are still successful.

Table 1 shows you the possible outcomes if you adopt 100% of these new mindset recommendations:

Table 1.1 - Overview *of Staying Power*

Mindset Shift To:	Action Outcome	No Action Outcome
Eliminating Vision Barriers	Growth & sustainability	Eventual business failure
Sharpening Your Vision	Growth & sustainability	Business suffocation leading to eventual failure
Welcoming Sacrifice	Growth & sustainability	Accepting failure and giving up on your dream(s)
Learning to Take Risks	Learning from mistakes and experience growth and sustainability	Playing it safe and eventually missing enough opportunities resulting in failure
Creating Something Out of Nothing	Growth & sustainability	Waiting and waiting while the business is faltering into failure
Drawing Up a Sustainability Road map	Growth, sustainability & piece of mind	Saying you owned a short-term cyclical business that simply failed

Where do I go if I need help?

- ROTB (Rule of Thumb for Business) - Website: (ruleofthumbbiz.com)
- SBA Small Business Development Centers – Website: (http://www.sba.gov/about-offices-content/1/2894)
- University Schools/College of Business (faculty and student interns)
- SCORE (Service Corps of Retired Executives)

Rule of Thumb:
Remember, this book is your desktop guide to small business sustainability; you will still need to surround yourself with business sustainability experts.

Chapter 2
Sustaining a Small Business:
Diversifying Revenues
How Can I Diversify Business Revenues?

If your business is like most businesses, you offer more than one product or service. For example, if you own an accounting firm, you likely offer monthly accounting services <u>and</u> prepare income tax returns for your clients and walk-ins who are not your clients. The money you collect for your services comes in peaks and valleys. Your highest months for revenues are probably January through April and again in October, when extended tax returns are due. The goal in business diversification is to bring in higher streams of money during what have traditionally been your slow months. Here are the known facts about small business revenues:

- Some months revenues are highly profitable and profit margins are high.
- Other months, revenues and profit margins are low or lacking.
- Some of the transactions are single (one-time).
- Other transactions are recurring (charging the same client month after month on a set fee

based on services delivered).

- Some of the services or products are unique; that is not traditionally offered by other firms in your industry code(s).
- Other services or products are replicas of what everyone else offers or sells and potential customers/clients can go elsewhere to find the same service or product available, often for lower prices, regardless of quality.

Diversifying your business revenue streams is another critically needed component for business sustainability.

Rule of Thumb:
Diversifying your business offerings results in diversifying your business revenues. You must differentiate your business from the rest of the pack.

How do I approach business diversification?

First, you must take an inventory of the products or services that you currently offer. They likely fall into one of the following traditional classifications:

Customary: These are the products or services that current or potential customers and clients expect you to provide or sell based on your industry. Example: My primary industry is technical writing and potential clients expect me to write their churn-out technical writing documents for them. Customary products or services bring in ongoing steady revenues.

Core: These are the products or services that represent a substantial amount of profit for your business. They may not be unique, but they are in high demand on a recurring basis. It's the first service that potential customers/clients think of when they hear or see the name of your business. Example: My core service is grant writing. The name Bev Browning & Associates is highly branded for providing top of the field services that lead to grant awards. Core products or services bring in ongoing steady revenues.

Complementary: These are products or services that would be considered *ala carte* on a food menu—the side dishes. Complementary products or services are not standalone or obvious revenue generators. Instead, they are the behind the scenes third-party vendors that add a needed ingredient to your business offerings. Example: A dry cleaners makes money for dry cleaning patrons' clothing or household items. However, if alterations or other sewing repairs are needed, the dry cleaner contracts with a third-party seamstress. Whatever the seamstress charges is included in the final bill for the customer. The dry cleaner marks up the third-party charge to capture overhead in addition to the actual cost of dry cleaning. Complementary products or services bring in steady revenues—smaller profit margins, but steady bank deposits.

Easy Entry: These are customer/client-baiting products or services. It's a low cost offering to get them in the door for the first time. The key to using the easy entry bait approach is to have a sales pitch ready for the rest of your products or services. Example: A bakery offers a cup of coffee for 39 cents one day a month to all customers who come in between 6 a.m. and 8 a.m. Remember, this is traditionally breakfast time. The likelihood of any cheap cup of coffee taker also buying one or more muffins, donuts, or other pastries is extremely high. The order of freshly baked food will draw in existing and new customers for the bakery. Easy entry products or services have a lower price and profit margin, but have a higher rate of sales.

Bundled: These are single products or services that are combined into a package offering. Customers/clients like bundles because they believe they are getting more for less. Example: Online shopping networks frequently offer a computer (at a higher price than the rest of the sales inventory) and give the customer a free printer, USB thumb drive, and bundled software—at no additional charge. The callers jump at getting a bundled deal. Bundled products or services should deal and produce high sales and profit margins.

Premium: These are products or services that command higher prices and emanate higher value. Example: Your cable television provider offers a premium channel selection; this is an upgrade from basic cable services. It's a unique attractive offering, so subscriptions soar. Premium products or services separate a business from its competitors because of perceived values.

Leveraged: These are products and services that generate revenues without time, people, and money. Example: e-Commerce sales on a how-to e-book, once written and digitalized for online upload and download, sells itself over and over without any additional drain on your business resources. Leveraged products or services make money for your business while you sleep. They create a low, but steady stream of revenues.

Recurring: These are products or services that repeat in pre-determined frequency. Example: House-cleaning services are delivered on a regularly scheduled basis. You can anticipate future revenues for existing clients based on the number of contracts signed and length of contracts. Recurring revenues are constant, known, and can be used to prove future income when a business applies for a bank loan or line of credit.

Rule of Thumb:
You've invested all of your assets into starting your business. Now, spend some time planting sustainability seeds.

The second way to approach business diversification is to take the eight classifications of business revenues and inventory your business's types of revenues for its products or services.

Table 2.1 – Revenue Type Analysis

Type of Revenue	In Place Yes or No?	Action Plan
Customary	Yes	Increase awareness
Core	Yes	Increase awareness
Complementary	No	Identify and add a third-party layer of services related to your current products or services.
Easy Entry	No	Explore a lower-priced product or service to get potentials customers in the door.
Bundled	No	Examine the complete list of products and services provided and create a bundled package (price lower than the total of single service or product offerings)
Premium	No	Look at what you currently have for sale and add an upgrade enhancement.
Leveraged	No	Brainstorm e-commerce information products or services that are automated for your business and the buyers. Think higher monthly revenues with little resource output.
Reoccurring	No	Explore how you can bring your one-purchase customer back again and again with recurring services, maintenance plans, or enhancement products.

Where do I go if I need help?

- ROTB (Rule of Thumb for Business) - Website: (ruleofthumbbiz.com)

- SBA Small Business Development Centers – Website: (http://www.sba.gov/about-offices-content/1/2894)
- University Schools/College of Business (faculty and student interns)
- SCORE (Service Corps of Retired Executives)

Chapter 3
Sustaining a Small Business:
Social Media Marketing
What is Social Media Marketing?

Social media marketing is the most talked about way for connecting one's business to the World Wide Web. It definitely elevates your business's visibility beyond the local zip code. What is social media marketing? Social media marketing refers to the process of gaining traffic or attention through social networking sites.

Social media marketing builds links that in turn support Search Engine Optimization (SEO) efforts. SEO is how your potential customers/clients find your Web site and learn about your products or services via the Internet. All major search engines such as Google, Yahoo and Bing have such results, where web pages and other content such as videos or local listings are shown and ranked based on what the search engine considers most relevant to users. Payment isn't involved, as it is with paid search ads. Small businesses that once only sold products or services in a local area are now selling those same revenue-driving products or services nationally and even internationally.

Social media does have a role in marketing, but that role depends on your industry and how it best fits the needs of your small business. It also depends on the effort you are willing to put forward when it comes to marketing via the most business-friendly social networks.

Is social media marketing the best approach for my business?

Marketing via the Internet has never been easier. Your next potential customer/client is just a mouse-click away. There are several social networking communities that can be used to network and promote your small business's products or services with thousands (no make that millions) of potential buyers. Social media marketing is another critically needed action to achieve business sustainability.

Where should I market my small business?

YouTube: Video. When it comes to marketing, video can be a great way to interact with potential customers, but you must do it correctly in order to attract new customers and not chase them away. They must see your video as providing them with interaction as well as value in order to be an effective means of social media marketing. According to social media marketing research, over 75% of the U.S. Internet audience views online videos. This accounts for 558 million hours of online video watching on a monthly basis. YouTube alone has over 258 million registered users, 50% of them visit weekly if not more. Are you seeing value yet? Small business owners know that they must be innovative and creative with marketing techniques and initiatives, so if you are not using YouTube, are you missing out? The short answer is yes.

Facebook: Posts, Advertising, Photos, and Chats. Most small business owners think of Facebook as a way to connect family and friends—and that was the initial use when it was created. However, today Facebook has become the hub for businesses promoting their products and services online. Consider the following statistics provided by O'Reilly Media. Between September 2008 and February 2009:

- Facebook users ages 26-34 increased by 26%
- Facebook users between the ages of 35 and 44 increased by 51%
- Facebook users among the ages 45-54 grew by 47%

Why should you use Facebook as a marketing tool? The answer is easy; you can use Facebook to gain new clients, stay in touch with current clients and promote new products and sales offers. You can also use it to create buzz and public relations (specifically) about your business.

How do you do this? Facebook offers you many tools to be successful in marketing your business, but you must have an understanding of these tools. First,

Facebook offers you Facebook Pages. You can use Facebook Pages to create and give your business its own profile on Facebook; the best thing is Facebook Pages is free. These pages give your business an identity on Facebook which strengthens your brand. Current customers or even potential customers can become fans of your page, and by doing so this allows them to follow you and receive any updates that you post to your page. Second, Facebook offers you Facebook Groups which is similar to Facebook Pages. The difference is they are built around a group of people rather than your business or your brand. You must be a member of Facebook to create a Facebook Group. In order to create a group, just log in to Facebook and then click on the Groups link in the main menu. You can use Facebook Groups to create awareness of your business. Example: Fans of Steve's Plumbing and Heating. You can use email to ask for satisfied customer testimonies and provide the link to your Facebook Groups page. This way, new customers can review testimonies on the link that you provide them to your Facebook Groups page.

Here are some others to maximize business visibility on Facebook:

- Promote your Facebook page offsite via other social network posts or tweets.
- Make your Facebook page interesting by adding a blog, notes, and photographs of

business events (ribbon cutting, news articles, employee events/meetings, and more).

- Have a clear idea of what you want your Facebook readers to do when they find your business's Facebook page. If you want to drive potential customers to your business Website, you have to add a link and post frequently about specials, discounts, and other info bits that will drive readers to want to read more on your Website.

- Use Facebook Ads to start your social media marketing campaign. They are cost-effective and will drive people towards your Facebook Pages.

- Make your Facebook Page content easy to share. Create a blog link back to your business Website. Once your potential customers are on your Website, create buttons for them to share the information or sales-related news with Facebook. You can also add buttons for Twitter and other social networking Websites.

- Give your Facebook fans exclusives (deals, sneak previews, and discounts).

- Use Facebook analytics to monitor the success of your page(s).

Twitter: Short Posts of 140 Characters or Less. Twitter is one of the fast-growing online platforms that is being used for communication and conversation.

Twitter has over one million users and broadcasts over three million messages every day. You can use Twitter to post news or updates about your business or products. However, please don't do this before you become familiar with the format and etiquette of Twitter. The best way to do this is to post a link to the full content of the news or update. Think of what's valuable to your consumers and let them hear about it first on Twitter. You'll be amazed how your following will grow. As you begin to use Twitter you will notice that it's all about conversation. It's about talking to your prospects and consumers, interacting with them. If you are not going to do this, don't use Twitter as a marketing tool, it simply won't work. Make friends, be a friend and reply. Show your followers that you want to engage and be involved with them.

LinkedIn: Posts, Business Listings, Advertising, Slide Share, Events, and Business Logo or Photo Options. Small businesses are using LinkedIn to find leads, grow their business globally, or find the right vendors. Here are some ways to use LinkedIn to increase your business revenues and start on the road to business sustainability:

- Acquire new customers through online recommendations and word of mouth.
- Keep in touch with people who care most about your business—previous customers and colleagues.

- Find the right vendors to outsource services you're not an expert on. Remember those complementary services in Chapter 2?
- Build your industry network—online and in person.
- Get answers to tough business questions with a little help from your real friends—other business owners.
- Win new business by answering questions in your area of expertise.
- Raise funding by connecting with venture capitalists.
- Network with peers in your industry for repeat business referrals.
- Convince potential customers of your expertise by sharing unique blog content.
- Keep your friends close and your competition closer. Learn what competitors are doing to attract new business.

Where do I go if I need help?

- ROTB (Rule of Thumb for Business) - Website: (ruleofthumbbiz.com)
- SBA Small Business Development Centers – Website: (http://www.sba.gov/about-offices-content/1/2894)
- University Schools/College of Business (faculty and student interns)
- SCORE (Service Corps of Retired Executives)

Chapter 4
Sustaining a Small Business: Branding
How Can I Brand My Small Business?

Branding isn't just about using your business logo or symbol in all of your advertising materials and business documents. The American Marketing Association (AMA) defines a brand as a "name, term, sign, symbol or design, or a combination of them intended to identify the goods and services of one seller or group of sellers and to differentiate them from those of other sellers." Therefore it makes sense to understand that branding is not about getting your target market to choose you over the competition, but it is about getting your prospects to see you as the only one that provides a solution to their problem. Branding is another critically needed component for business sustainability.

The objectives that a good brand will achieve include:
- Delivers the message clearly
- Confirms your credibility
- Connects to your target prospects emotionally
- Motivates the buyer
- Concretes user loyalty

To succeed in branding you must understand the needs and wants of your customers and prospects. You do this by integrating your brand strategies throughout your business at every point of public contact. Your brand resides within the hearts and minds of customers, clients, and prospects. It is the sum total of their experiences and perceptions, some of which you can influence, and some that you cannot. A strong brand is invaluable as the battle for customers intensifies day by day. It's important to spend time investing in researching, defining, and building your brand in order to create a brand strategy. After all, your brand is the source of a promise to your consumer. It's a foundational piece in your marketing communication and one you do not want to be without. Your brand strategy is a multi-layered name and visual recognition approach to increasing your market share for the products or services you sell, manufacture, or distribute.

How can I define my business's brand?

This is the first step in the process of developing your brand strategy. By defining who your brand is, you create the foundation for all other components to build on. Your brand definition will serve as your measuring stick in evaluating any and all marketing materials and strategies. You will begin this process by answering the questions on the next page.

1. What products and/or services do you offer? Define the qualities of these services and/or products.

2. What are the core values of your products and services? What are the core values of your business?

3. What is the mission of your business?

4. What does your business specialize in?

5. Who is your target market? Who do your products and services attract?

6. What is the tagline (advertising slogan) of your business? What message does your tagline send to your prospective customers/clients?

7. Using the information in Steps 1 through 6 (above), create a personality or character for your business that represents your products or services. What is the character like? What qualities stand out? Is the personality of your business innovative, creative, energetic, or sophisticated?

8. Use the personality that you created in the previous step and build a relationship with your target market that you defined in Step 5. How does that personality react to the target audience? What characteristics stand out? Which characteristics and qualities get the attention of your prospects?

9. Review the answers to Steps 7 and 8 to create a profile of your brand. Describe the personality

or character with words just as if you were writing a biography or personal advertisement. Be creative! The results of Steps 1 through 9 create your business's brand.

Where do I go if I need help?

- ROTB (Rule of Thumb for Business) - Website: (ruleofthumbbiz.com)
- American Marketing Association – Website: (www.marketingpower.com)
- SBA Small Business Development Centers – Website: (http://www.sba.gov/about-offices-content/1/2894)
- University Schools/College of Business (faculty and student interns)
- SCORE (Service Corps of Retired Executives)

Chapter 5
Sustaining a Small Business: Networking
How Can I Use Networking to
Increase Revenues?

Just hanging up your business sign, getting it listed in the Yellow Pages, and printing some business cards will not result in business sustainability. Who will know about your location, products or services, pride in ownership? Who will spread the word about how great your products or services are? Will the first customer to walk in the door be looking for directions elsewhere? Getting customers/clients is not an easy process without all of the right marketing tools and strategies in place to drive people in your door or to your Website. Networking—getting out and attending meetings where you have potential customers, current customers, business owners, and government officials—is critical to reaching business sustainability.

What types of networks can I promote my small business in?

Chamber of Commerce. The U.S. Chamber of Commerce is the world's largest business federation, representing 3 million businesses of all sizes, sectors, and regions, as well as state and local chambers and industry associations. More than 96% of U.S. Chamber members are small businesses with 100 employees or fewer. Becoming a member of your local or regional Chamber of Commerce can help you promote your business's brand, attract new business, and identify complementary services (Remember those complementary services in Chapter 2?) Your membership buys you access to the Chamber's business directory; a Web page on the Chamber's Web site, and multiple other free marketing and branding opportunities. By hosting one of the monthly Business to Business (B2B) networking events, you allow Chamber members and visitors to see your products or services firsthand. This is the best word of mouth advertising possible, and over time, it will increase your business revenues.

State Business Associations and Networks. The best way to find out if your state has a small business association network (for example: Arizona Small Business Association) is to contact your closest Small Business Administration or Small Business Development Centers' Network. These state-based associations or networks have monthly member meetings that include professional development training, social interacting, and new business presentations. Don't miss out on this type of networking opportunity.

Business Network International (BNI). The group is the world's largest referral organization. A big claim, but given the number of successful people who pay good money to belong, it must be worthwhile. Local chapters usually meet once a week and are limited to one person per profession. BNI provides the opportunity to share ideas, contacts and most importantly, referrals. Members are expected to provide others with referrals and get a chance to showcase their own services.

How can these networks help me achieve business sustainability?

You must view networking as a marketing tool that requires a strategic approach. You can't just wake up, run out of the door, and attend an early morning networking meeting without a plan for success. Here are some tips to help you maximize each networking event:

- **Appearance.** Dress like you want new business. Don't attend in denim or casual attire. Do something with your hair; don't just wake up, shake your head and dash off to begin the day. Make an impression; leave an impression and your phone will start to ring more often.
- **Early Bird Reputation.** Arrive early and speak with the host of the networking group. Get to know the host and ask for information

about other members (before they arrive). Use this technique to make the most of your networking time when members arrive. Advance information is power; learn who you need to align with in order to take your business to a higher level.

- **Business Cards.** Always carry lots of business cards in your car, briefcase, purse, and pocket. Why? Give them out to everyone you meet, from the waiter or receptionist or registration person at the networking meeting site to every person you shake hands with or just speak casually with—impress by using higher quality business cards, not the ones printed out at home! Handing out business cards is the ultimate action in networking. Of course, if you don't have an effective data management process in place, the business cards are useless. More about data management at the end of this chapter.

- **Name Tag.** Don't depend on horrible peel-off, adhesive-back name tags given out by the networking site host. Have a custom name tag created with your branding identification (colors, name of business, your name, phone number, and a logo). Make sure that your name tag is at last 2″ x 2″ in size. Make it easy for the trifocal wearers to see who you are and the name of your business from across the room. Have several name tags made up (5 is the magic number) and place them in your car's glove compartment; in your purse or briefcase; one by the door you use when you leave home and head to your business, and one next to your daily jewelry choices. This way, even if you forget that you have a networking meeting that day, you still have your *branding* sign on your lapel! Help potential customers remember who you are and help them remember the name of your business. You'll get more business referrals and make more dollars.

- **Event Sponsorship.** All networking groups need a place to meet; While some groups have a regular meeting place (restaurant or public meeting space in a city hall or chamber of commerce), for special occasions (holiday season), meeting at a private business is a great idea. You can volunteer your business place (providing you have the meeting and mingling space) or opt to sponsor free drinks or appetizers. The sponsoring business usually gets a lot of publicity before and during the event. This is a good way to drive new business opportunities to you.

- **Networking Directory Inclusion.** Most networking groups have a member directory (hard paper copy or online). Once you're a member, you can list your business in the directory. This is a benefit that typically comes with your membership dues. It's a great way to let other networking members, especially those who are members but do not attend regularly or at the same location that you go to for your meetings, about your business. People will remember you and refer potential customers/clients to your business.

What are the action steps to power networking?

Like any small business owner, time spent away from your business causes you to lose money. You want to make the best use of your networking time and add to your profit margin via networking. Here are some power networking action steps to keep you focused:

- **Step 1 - Move Fast.** Introduce yourself to as many networking members as possible.
- **Step 2 - Use a Script.** Have a 30-second script to introduce you and your business. Share a snippet of free information. For example, if you're a collection agency, tell them the percent of small businesses that have to use collection agencies. Plant a seed. Also, talk about the dollars collected percent and return on investment for your customers/clients.
- **Step 3 - Get the Data.** Ask each person you meet for their business card. Keep all cards in

one place until you get back to your business. Scan them for email, telephone, and mail campaigns. This is Data Management and it's critical. Don't just collect cards to throw away or toss into a file drawer. You build your referral network and new customer/client base from timely and diligent data management.

- **Step 4 - Follow-Up.** People have short memories. Follow up regularly with members of your network or they'll forget you exist, and more importantly, they will forget that you are the best person to solve their problems or meet their needs. Contact the people in your network at least once a month.

Where do I go if I need help?

- ROTB (Rule of Thumb for Business) - Website: (ruleofthumbbiz.com)
- U.S. Chamber of Commerce – Website: (http://www.uschamber.com/chambers/directory)
- Business Network International – Website: (http://www.bni.com)
- Vistaprint – Website: (http://www.vistaprint.com)

Chapter 6
Sustaining a Small Business:
Contract Bidding Opportunities
How Can I Use Contract Bidding
to Increase Revenues?

It's amazing how many small businesses are not aware of contract bidding opportunities or how to find them via the Internet. No business owner starts a business with the vision of having it fail. Yet, looking at other revenue options only occurs when the business is already failing. As long as money is coming in the door and cash register, an enemy called complacency sets in quickly. Don't let your business be another victim of failing to think outside of the box. Finding and pursuing contract bidding opportunities is a critical component to business sustainability.

How do I find contract bidding opportunities for my business?

There are several bid services that you can Google on the Internet. Here's a quick overview of what's out there and the likely cost range:

- **Bid Net.** BidNet's Web site says it has helped thousands of companies to grow with government opportunities. Their subscription based service has more than 87,000 agencies across all levels of the government that publish bids for the products and services they need to buy and bidders' lists with interested suppliers and contract award details. BidNet does not advertise its rates on their Website. However, as a personal subscriber through one of my current contractors, I can tell you that rates start at $2,000 and up for national bid alert services.

- **Find RFP.** This bid search service is subscription-based. Find RFP maintains a comprehensive database of government RFPs (government RFP, Request for Proposal), government bids, government contracts, RFQs (RFQ, Request for Quotations), and RFIs (RFI, Request for Information) published by federal, state, county, city, municipal, local government, town agencies, and government agency buyers such as colleges, universities, school districts, hospitals, correctional facilities, water districts, public utilities, police and fire departments. There are two subscription plans, National (all 50 states for under $30 monthly) and Regional (up to four states for under $20 monthly).

- **Google Alerts.** It's not true about free things being less than high quality. I'm impressed with Google Alerts. You specify the query or queries you'd like Google to monitor. As Google searches the Internet, if it finds a change that you've asked to be notified about — that is, one of your Alerts — you'll get an email message. Google will tell you about new results once a week, once a day, or as soon as they're found. (You won't necessarily get a message every day or week. Google only sends email if there's something new to report.) Example: you are an accountant and you want to bid on work outside of your local area. Simply set up several Google alerts to hit the target for finding contract bidding opportunities. Here's the trick to fine-tuning your Google Alerts:

○ RFP for accountant + your state name.

○ RFP for accountant + national

(yes, type the word national)

○ RFQ for accountant + your state name.

○ RFQ for accountant + national

○ Request for accounting services + your state name.

○ Request for accounting services + national.

○ Contract bid opportunities + accounting + current month and year (January 2012).

Using my search term examples, you would need to set up seven Google Alerts. You can probably think of a lot more terms to use to capture all possible contract bidding opportunities.

State, Regional and Local Procurement Agencies. Don't forget to check the Internet to see if your state, county, or city has published procurement opportunities. Often these contract bidding announcements will be on the purchasing department's Website or in a secure (register, use a log-in and password) Web page or site where the bid letting agency can track who's pulling out bids.

Does a very small business have a chance of winning a bid?

If you're a sole proprietor, you may want to consider upgrading your business structure to a corporation (C corp., S corp, or Limited Liability Corporation – LLC). The majority of bid-letting agencies require that potential vendors register with the state or county or city before submitting bids for products or services. These agencies all ask for you Federal Employer Identification Number (EIN) and your Data Universal Numbering System (DUNS) number. Even a very small business must present itself as a big, experienced and capable business in order to win contract bids.

Another possibility is that you could look at the list of previous contract awards in your industry code area and contact them to see if they are planning to re-bid on the opportunity. If they are, you can propose that your business be a subcontractor under their contract to provide complementary services (remember to check back with Chapter 2 to understand complementary services). Being a subcontractor will get your business in the door with the bid-letting agency and bring in steady dollars for your business. Example: You own a very small upholstery and leather repair business. The County has just released a bid for 5,000 new chairs to install in the convention center. You monitor the County's procurement Website to see who is attending the bidder's conference (yes, large scale contract opportunities require public bidder's conferences where interested parties can ask questions about the RFP's requirements). Once you know who's going to be there, you go too! After the session, meet with one or two of the companies planning to bid on the chair order. Indicate that you can provide ongoing maintenance on the chairs as a complementary service to their bid. Remember, the bidder that presents the most comprehensive and cost-effective bid response package will win the bid. Now you will have work for upwards to 3 to 5 years to provide ongoing chair repairs. Think outside of the box!

Where do I go if I need help?
- ROTB (Rule of Thumb for Business) - Website: (ruleofthumbbiz.com)

- SBA Small Business Development Centers – Website: (http://www.sba.gov/about-offices-content/1/2894)
- FindRFP – Website (http://www.findrfp.com)
- Google Alerts – Website: (http://www.google.com/alerts)

Chapter 7
Sustaining a Small Business: Finances
How Can I Find Money for My Business?

If I had $100 for every business visionary that called me to inquire about start-up or expansion funds, I would be living on an island and resting; not writing a new book. However, as a small business owner for nearly 40 years, I too wanted to know about all available funding. The results of my research will give you promise, but may also make you think longer about where you get your business start-up or expansion funds from. Remember, money will only come to you and your business if you aggressively look for it on an ongoing basis. Finding the cash needed to make it through a slow month or year is critical to your small business's sustainability.

How can I find grants for my small business?

Many unscrupulous entities falsely taut, via the media, that there are government grants to start your business. They fail to tell you who is eligible for the grants and the process for qualifying for a grant as a for-profit (money making) business. Here are some very reliable resources to get you started on legitimate small business grant information Websites:

U.S. Small Business Administration. The federal government does NOT provide grants for starting and expanding a business.

Government grants are funded by your tax dollars and therefore require very stringent compliance and reporting measures to ensure the money is well spent. As you can imagine, grants are not given away indiscriminately.

Grants from the federal government are only available to non-commercial organizations, such as non-profits and educational institutions in areas such as medicine, education, scientific research, and technology development. The federal government also provides grants to state and local governments to assist them with economic development.

Some business grants are available through state and local programs, non-profit organizations, and other groups. For example, some states provide grants for expanding child care centers, creating energy efficient technology, and developing marketing campaigns for tourism. These grants are not necessarily free money, and usually require the recipient to match funds or combine the grant with other forms of financing such as a loan. The amount of the grant money available varies with each business and each grantor.

If you are not one of these specialized businesses, both federal and state government agencies provide financial assistance programs that help small business owners obtain low-interest loans and venture capital financing from commercial lenders.

How can I find loans for my small business?

U.S. Small Business Administration. If you're planning to start a business or expand an existing business, you might need financing help. SBA participates in a number of loan programs designed for business owners who may have trouble qualifying for a traditional bank loan.

To start the process, you should visit a local bank or lending institution that participates in SBA programs. SBA loan applications are structured to meet SBA requirements, so that the loan is eligible for an SBA guarantee. This guarantee represents the portion of the loan that SBA will repay to the lender if you default on your loan payments.

The SBA Loan Application Checklist provides a listing of forms and documents you and your lender will need to create a loan package to submit to SBA. On their Website, the following loan listings are direct links to information about commonly requested SBA programs.

Starting and Expanding Businesses

* Basic 7(a) Loan Program
  Provides growing businesses with long-term, fixed-rate financing for major fixed assets, such as land and buildings.

47

- Certified Development Company (CDC) 504 Loan Program
Offers very small loans to start up, newly established or growing small business concerns. SBA makes funds available to nonprofit community-based lenders which, in turn, make loans to eligible borrowers in amounts up to a maximum of $35,000. Applications are submitted to the local intermediary and all credit decisions are made on the local level.

- Microloan Program
Provides small, short-term loans for small business concerns and certain types of not-for-profit child-care centers. The SBA makes funds available to specially designated intermediary lenders, which are nonprofit community-based organizations with experience in lending as well as management and technical assistance. These intermediaries make loans to eligible borrowers. The maximum loan amount is $50,000, but the average microloan is about $13,000. Microloans may be used for the following purposes: working capital; purchase of inventory or supplies; purchase of furniture or fixtures, and machinery or equipment. Proceeds from a microloan cannot be used to pay existing debts or to purchase real estate.

<u>Disaster Loans</u>

- Disaster Assistance Loans
  Assist small businesses, small agricultural
  cooperatives and nonprofit organizations as
  they recover from economic losses resulting
  from physical disaster or an agricultural
  production disaster.

- Economic Injury Loans
  If your business is located in a declared
  disaster area and has suffered economic injury
  because of the disaster (regardless of physical
  damage), you may be eligible for an Economic
  Injury Disaster Loan (EIDL). Substantial
  economic injury is the inability of a business to
  meet its obligations as they mature and to pay
  its ordinary and necessary operating expenses.
  EIDLs provide the necessary working capital
  to help small businesses survive until normal
  operations resume after a disaster.

<u>Export Assistance Loans</u>

- Export Express
  Offers loans targeted at businesses that are able
  to generate export sales but need additional
  working capital to support these opportunities.

- Export Working Capital
  Gives term loans that are designed for
  businesses that plan to start/continue exporting
  or those that that have been adversely affected

by competition from imports. The proceeds of the loan must enable the borrower to be in a better position to compete.

- International Trade Loans
  The International Trade Loan Program offers term loans to businesses that plan to start or continue exporting, or that have been adversely affected by competition from imports. The proceeds of the loan must enable the borrower to be in a better position to compete. The program offers borrowers a maximum SBA-guaranteed portion of $1.75 million.

Veteran and Military Community Loans

- Patriot Express Pilot Loan Initiative
  Offers funds to eligible small businesses to meet ordinary and necessary operating expenses that could have been met, but are unable to meet, because an essential employee was "called-up" to active duty in their role as a military reservist.
- Military Reservist Economic Injury
  Disaster Loan
  Provides funds to eligible small businesses to meet ordinary and necessary operating expenses that it could have met, but was unable to meet, because an essential employee

was "called-up" to active duty in their role as a military reservist.

Special Purpose Loans

- Pollution Control Loans
  Provides financing to eligible small businesses for the planning, design or installation of a pollution control facility.
- U.S. Community Adjustment and Investment Program (CAIP)
  Assists U.S. companies that are doing business in areas of the country that have been negatively affected by the North American Free Trade Agreement (NAFTA). To be eligible, a business must reside in a county noted as being negatively affected by NAFTA, based on job losses and the unemployment rate of the county.

How can I locate state-level grant or loan options?

The SBA has conveniently created a Web page to find financing for your small business. Depending on where your business operates, each state will have different options for grants (or loans). Just fill in the online form and hit search. Here is the link for the online search form: http://www.sba.gov/content/search-business-loans-grants-and-financing.

How can I find venture capital for my small business?

Venture capital is a type of equity financing that addresses the funding needs of entrepreneurial companies that for reasons of size, assets, and stage of development cannot seek capital from more traditional sources, such as public markets and banks. Venture capital investments are generally made as cash in exchange for shares and an active role in the invested company.

The New Markets Venture Capital Companies

The New Markets Venture Capital (NMVC) program seeks to stimulate economic development in Low Income (LI) areas. [Through public-private partnerships between the SBA and newly formed NMVC Companies (NMVCCs) and existing Specialized Small Business Investment Companies (SSBICs), the program is designed to serve the unmet equity needs of local entrepreneurs through developmental venture capital investments, provide technical assistance to small businesses, create quality employment opportunities for LI area residents, and build wealth within LI areas.]

All SBIC Licensees by State

The Small Business Investment Company (SBIC) Program provides venture capital to small businesses. Although SBICs are licensed and regulated by SBA, they are private, profit-seeking investment companies. There is an online directory on the SBA's Web site to

locate an SBIC in your state. Here is the link: http://
www.sba.gov/content/all-sbic-licensees-state.

Where do I go if I need help?

- ROTB (Rule of Thumb for Business) - Website:
  (ruleofthumbbiz.com)
- U.S. Small Business
  Administration/Grants – Website:
  (http://www.sba.gov/category/navigation-
  structure/starting-managing-business/starting-
  business/loans-grants-funding/grants)
- U.S. Small Business
  Administration/Loans – Website:
  (http://www.sba.gov/content/sba-loans)
- SBA Small Business
  Development Centers – Website:
  (http://www.sba.gov/about-offices-content/1/2894)

Chapter 8
Sustaining a Small Business: Reinvention
How Can I Meet Emerging Service
or Product Demands?

If you own a retail outlet or grocery store, you know how important it is to rotate stock on the shelf, move things around, and make your entire inventory look different, fresh, and unique. If you're in manufacturing, you know that when models change, the entire assembly line must be retrofitted to produce the latest and the greatest. But what happens when your business stops getting orders and workers must be laid off or cut back on their hours? How do you handle this situation? What if you're a real estate broker and houses are no longer selling, what can you do to keep your business going financially? Knowing how to reinvent your services or products before the money stops flowing in is critical to sustaining your small business.

How do I know when it's time to reinvent my services or products?

Here are some warning signs of business stagnation and decline:

- **Feedback from Customers/Clients.** When you start hearing questions like: Do you have anything else? When will something new be in? Are you offering any more services? Have you thought about branching out? Clue after clue, the writing is on the wall. If you don't reinvent your business in some form or manner, you will not have a demand for you to supply much longer. Take feedback seriously and begin to plan for and implement change throughout your business if you want to stay in business.

- **Decline in Revenues.** A small business owner should always keep an eye on the bottom line. It could be fatal if you only compared sales peaks and valleys once a year in a 45-minute meeting with your accountant. If you use accounting software, you are able to compare sales from day to day, week to week, month to month, and year to year. You can also identify the peaks and valleys and connect them with specific marketing efforts. You can even create an Excel spreadsheet to track sales trends. If you know that every year during June, July and August, your school supply business soars, but from September through December, sales are low, you can create special marketing events during the slow months. You can also use these slow months to participate in trade shows, conferences, or even create your own training program about how to purchase school supplies wisely. Even a blog on this topic will help parents—your primary buyers.

- **Entrepreneurial Intuition.** You started your business based on intuition, knowledge, and ability. You knew the right time to launch, what to sell or provide, and how to drive services or products from the concept phase to the reality phase—selling them and collecting revenues. When you get that sinking feeling that you won't be able to keep the doors open much longer, it won't be when you're ready to close the doors. It will be when you first recognize that you must shift your mindset and come up with more ideas to bring dollars in the door. Always trust your intuition. It's what got you started and it's what will help you move wisely to sustain your business.

What are the steps to reinventing what I've always done?

Step 1: Be aware of and analyze your financial situation daily. Look at sales receipts, expenses, and profit margins. Know where the red flags are and make a running list of red flags (problems) and how to remove them (solutions). If you have to use a large white board on the wall in your office, all the better. You'll be able to update it daily and it will be glaring at you every time you enter your office. It will demand reflections, planning, and actions.

Step 2: Explore your possibilities. First, brainstorm with yourself. Ask: What can I do or sell? What do I know that I'm not using in my business? What can I learn in order to add a new service? What new complementary products can I carry that buyers will always purchase somewhere else. Example: You specialize in selling Amish furniture. Your entire store is Amish furniture. However, when someone comes in and buys a dining room set, they usually will need a tablecloth, a vase or other centerpiece, and cloth napkins for special occasions. Find some space in your building to create an Amish closet corner where you can start to carry these uniquely created items. Your new inventory will complement what you already sell and you know have specialty items for holidays and special occasions. Think outside of the box—all day, every day!

Step 3: Develop reinvention goals and benchmarks. By this, I mean that you must write down specific outcome goals for each new idea. Example: I'm a grant writer by trade. However, when business is slow (it happens yearly), I look for new ways to grow my skills and become an expert in unfamiliar areas. Here is my reinvention goal: Write a book on business sustainability and target small businesses. Benchmark: By the end of this year, 100% of the new book, *Rule of Thumb – Sustainability for Small Businesses*, will be completed and bringing in new royalty revenues. Here's another goal: Become an expert in the grant management process and develop a new workshop training series. Benchmark(s): By the first quarter of next year, complete 100% of the requirements for the grant management certification. By the third quarter of next year, develop a grant management training curriculum, create a Website, and schedule five or more training events. If my business as a grant writer is dying, I can reinvent myself into an expert on grant management. It's worth a try; the risk is minimal, and I just might create a new revenue stream from the book and the trainings.

Step 4: Document the process for ongoing replication. It's not easy to continually reinvent yourself. As a writer, I work hard to reinvent myself every year; sometimes, several times per year. I keep a business journal on failed ideas and new ideas. I note what works and what does not work. Just in case I become so consumed and stressed over getting new business that I forget how I reinvented myself two years ago, I can re-read the journal and the excitement of change begins to set in.

Where do I go if I need help?

- ROTB (Rule of Thumb for Business) - Website: (ruleofthumbbiz.com)
- SBA Small Business Development Centers – Website: (http://www.sba.gov/about-offices-content/1/2894)
- University Schools/College of Business (faculty and student interns)
- SCORE (Service Corps of Retired Executives)

Chapter 9
Sustaining a Small Business: Succession
How Can I Plan for Succession?

What is business succession? A well thought out plan for long-term business sustainability. When you are ready to retire or become ill or simply want to work less than 24 hours a day, seven days a week, you will need to have a plan in place for who will take over the business and keep it going. Even if you're not active any longer, you can still draw money from the revenues as the founder or advisor to the new manager. Keep this in mind, you will always be the owner; you just won't be as active. Don't we all want to plant the seeds that will grow over time so we can still enjoy the beauty of what we started from afar?

What can a business succession plan do for me?

Whether you choose to transfer out of your current role or leave the business altogether, a business succession plan can help ensure the orderly transfer of ownership - to your partners, other family members or your heirs. Most financial planners offer business succession planning services to help you think through the business management transition as well as the financial realities if you're no longer actively focusing on sustainability and when you're no longer visible to long-time customers/clients when they walk into your business. Both of these scenarios could easily cause drastic drops in sales or services revenue.

Succession planning experts can work with you to carry out estate planning, transitioning ownership, and determine the tax advantages for all succession options explored. In short, succession planning can ease your mind about the future (aka sustainability) of the business that you lost sleep and time over when you were first starting out on this entrepreneurial adventure.

Where do I go if I need help?

- ROTB (Rule of Thumb for Business) - Website: (ruleofthumbbiz.com)
- Independent Directory of Financial Advisors – Website: (http://www.allfinancialadvisors.com/)
- Financial Planning Association – Website: (http://www.fpanet.org/PlannerSearch/Members/default.aspx)
- Family Business Succession Planning – Website: (http://sbinfocanada.about.com/cs/buysellabiz/a/succession1_2.htm)
- Succession Planning Template and Guide – Web link: (www.business.gov.au/Documents/Successionplantemplateandguide.doc)

Conquering The Basics

As you can see from the information in *Rule of Thumb: A Guide to Sustainability for Small Business*, keeping a small business operating takes a lot of know-how. The information in this book gives you the basic steps you must follow to sustain your business, as well as information plans for business sustainability.

As a business owner, you will need to keep a number of critical facts in mind. The following are reminders of some basic information, of which you may need to remind yourself when stress overtakes common sense and you place an order for 1,000 pet rocks (well, you know what I mean):

- Thinking about and planning for business sustainability takes a great amount of forethought, vision, and energy.
- Brainstorming to find ways to diversify your business revenues forces you to become creative and think outside of the box. While not always a comfortable process, it is nonetheless critical to sustainability.

- Understanding and using social media marketing networks to promote your business must be a daily priority.
- Becoming a savvy brander for your business must be a daily priority.
- Becoming an active business-to-business networker requires time and effort; however, visual recognition drives new customers/clients to your business.
- Aggressively going after contract bidding opportunities is critical to diversifying your business revenues.
- Reinventing your products or services successfully requires diligent monitoring and tracking of finances.
- Transitioning out of your business and still receiving revenues requires formal financial succession planning.

When you need additional answers that are not in this book, take the time and effort to find resources that will answer your questions. The appendix of this book offers some suggestions for additional resources. As the author of this book, I wish you great success in all of your business endeavors. Take the information that *Rule of Thumb: A Guide to Sustainability for Small Business* offers you, apply it, and get started on sustaining your successful business.

Additional Resources

The following is a list of resources that may provide answers to additional questions you may have about sustaining your small business.

- Local Chambers of Commerce
- Local business organizations
- Local trade unions related to your business
- Micro business loan organizations in your area
- State Chambers of Commerce
- Regional Community Development Corporations
- State Economic Development and Commerce Departments Home Pages: http://www.eda.gov/Resources/StateLinks.xml - National Association of State Development Agencies
- National Association of Seed and Venture Capital Funds: http://www.nasvf.org/
- Community Development Venture Capital Alliance: http://www.cdvca.org/
- Active Capital: http://activecapital.org/ assists local businesses connect with private capital: http://activecapital.org/nation
- USDA Rural Development State and Local Offices: http://www.rurdev.usda.gov/recd_map.html

Author Biography

Dr. Beverly A. Browning has been consulting in the areas of grant writing, contract bid responses, and organizational development for nearly four decades. Her clients have included small businesses, Fortune 500 corporations, chambers of commerce, faith-based organizations, units of local and county municipal governments, state and federal government agencies, school districts and colleges, social and human service agencies, hospitals, fire departments, and service associations.

Dr. Browning has assisted clients and workshop participants throughout the United States in receiving awards of more than $350 million. She is the author of 40 grants-related publications, including Grant Writing For Dummies™, Grant Writing for Educators, How to Become a Grant Writing Consultant, Faith-Based Grants: Aligning Your Church to Receive Abundance, Perfect Phrases for Writing Grant Proposals and

65

Perfect Phrases for Fundraising. Most recently, she used her decades of entrepreneurial experience to author A Guide to Sustainability for Small Business, a publication in the Rule of Thumb book series.

Dr. Browning holds degrees in Organizational Development, Public Administration, and Business Administration. She is a grant-writing course developer and online facilitator for Ed2Go.com. Dr. Browning's online courses (taught to thousands of students annually) are Advanced Proposal Writing and Becoming a Grant Writing Consultant. She is a current member of the Grant Professionals Association and Founder and Director of the Grant Writing Training. In 2011, she accepted the position of Vice President for Grants Professional Services at eCivis Inc. (www.ecivis.com).

Connect with Dr. Bev:
PHONE: 480-768-7400
EMAIL: grantsconsulting@aol.com
WEBSITES: www.bevbrowning.com and
www.grantwritingbootcamp.us
LINKEDIN: www.linkedin.com/in/bevbrowning
TWITTER: https://twitter.com/grantdoctor
DUMMIES BLOG:
grantwritingfordummies.wordpress.com/
FACEBOOK: https://www.facebook.com/
GrantWritingTrainingFoundation

Rule of Thumb
Small Business Book Series

Please enjoy these other titles from the Rule of Thumb for Business book series!

A Small Business Guide to Sales Strategy

Author: Jill Slupe

This book shares practical methods that can be used to accelerate sales in business. It leads new and existing business owners through the sales process and lays the groundwork for a sound sales strategy that serves as a foundation for successful business. Strategic and tactical exercises push the reader to create actual business strategies that drive revenue. Book ISBN: 978-1-60808-060-1

A Small Business Guide to Customer Service and Relationships

Author: Lisa Tschauner

This book is designed as a tool for the small business owner. Through identifying customers, their needs and wants, successful communication strategies, methods for follow-up and best practices, anyone who is involved in a business environment can build outstanding and valuable relationships with customers and clients. Readers will be guided through the developing dynamic and unique strategies that are sure to grow their business. Book ISBN: 978-1-60808-066-3

A Small Business Guide to Basics

Authors: Marian Shalander Kaiser and Michael Mitilier

As the initial book in the series, this guide will assist you in gaining a basic understanding of what it takes to operate a small business. It discusses the legal requirements, financial resources, record-keeping requirements, ways to market the business, communication skills, human resource laws, as well as issues that may arise on a day-to-day basis. Book ISBN: 978-1-60808-024-3

A Small Business Guide to Marketing
Author: David Catalan

This is an introductory guide for the first-time entrepreneur starting a new small business, as well as for an existing business owner who wants to grow and needs marketing advice. The author describes the essential, need-to-know concepts which combine to drive strategic directions toward success. Real world and commonly understood examples and experiences help the reader identify the strengths which underscore a healthy marketing business plan. Book ISBN: 978-1-60808-047-2

A Small Business Guide to Growth
Author: Linda Swalling Fettig

Business growth is an exciting and often very hectic time in the life cycle of a business. This easy to read book helps entrepreneurs understand business growth and the impact it has. Readers will learn how to work "on" their business even as they are busy working "in" their business. Book ISBN: 978-1-60808-062-5

A Small Business Guide to Marketing Yourself for Success

Author: Rita Rocker

In today's competitive business environment, good manners, proper speech patterns, a dynamic appearance, professional communication and networking skills can make the difference between getting ahead and being left behind. Readers will learn how to build a successful, personal brand, NOW!
Book ISBN: 978-1-60808-048-9

A Small Business Guide to Communication Basics for Owners and Managers

Author: Marian Shalander Kaiser

This book provides basic information to help you improve both written and oral communication skills. It shows you how to be kind to your readers by making what you've written easy to understand. Book ISBN: 978-1-60808-046-5

A Small Business Guide to Sustainability
Author: Dr. Beverly Ann Browning

This title closes the "how-to stay in business" information gap for micro and small businesses that are struggling to last beyond today's reactive approaches. It is for readers who have a vision of their business lasting forever. This guide show the action steps for diversifying revenues, lasting in the social media market, branding smarter, finding new revenue streams, and planning for business succession. Book ISBN: 978-1608080533

A Small Business Guide to Peak Performance Through People
Author: Todd Conkright

This brief guide provides practical insights that any manager of people will find useful. It introduces a simple process to ensure your organization achieves peak performance by selecting, managing and developing individuals who are aligned with your organization's goals. Book ISBN: 978-1608080779

The Rule of Thumb for Business book series is a collective of expert advice and guidance from industry professionals. These authors include the some of the best minds in today's business world. The books are easy to read and full of applicable information that will benefit any entrepreneur, manager or business leader.

Please visit the Rule of Thumb for Business website at www.ruleofthumbbiz.com to learn more information about this organization, contact us or to order additional books. The Rule of Thumb authors are also available for speaking engagements, conference workshops or for educational training purposes. Details and contact information for each author can be found on the website.

CPSIA information can be obtained
at www.ICGtesting.com
Printed in the USA
FFOW03n2241070414
4699FF